My Healthy Body
Fit and Well

Veronica Ross

Belitha Press

First published in the UK in 2002 by

Belitha Press
A member of **Chrysalis** Books plc
64 Brewery Road, London N7 9NT

ISBN 1 84138 406 2

British Library Cataloguing in Publication Data
for this book is available from the British Library.

Design: Bean Bog Frag Design
Picture researcher: Terry Forshaw
Consultant: Carol Ballard

Printed in Taiwan

10 9 8 7 6 5 4 3 2 1

(T) = Top, (B) = Bottom, (L) = Left, (R) = Right.

Picture acknowledgements:
All Photography by Claire Paxton with the exception of:
6 © Bubbles/Loisjoy Thurston; 7 © Bubbles/Frans Rombout;
17 © Medipics; 19 © Science Photo Library/Eye of Science; 23
© Bubbles/Jennie Woodcock; 24 © Bubbles/Dr. Hercules
Robinson; 28 © Bubbles/Peter Sylent; 29 © Bubbles/
Jennie Woodcock.

Contents

All about you

Bodies come in all shapes and sizes. Some are tall, some are short, some are fat and some are thin. You will use your body all your life so it is important to look after it.

No one looks just like you. Everyone is different. This makes you special.

Your body is made up of many different parts. How many can you name?

What colour are your eyes? Is your hair long or short, dark or fair?

head

hair

neck

shoulder

chest

elbow

finger

hand

hip

thigh

knee

leg

ankle

foot

toes

Body care

You need to look after your body to stay fit and well. You should try to eat three meals a day and drink lots of water. You also need to get plenty of rest.

Food gives you the energy you need to work and play.

Your body grows and repairs itself while you are asleep.

Looking after your body also means keeping it clean.

Keeping fit

There are lots of ways you can keep fit. Playing ball games and swimming will exercise your muscles. This will make your lungs and heart work better.

Can you lie on your back and pretend to ride a bicycle?

8

Which parts of your body do you use when you are playing ball games?

Walking is a good way to keep fit. Do you like walking to the park and the shops?

9

Time for exercise

You probably get lots of exercise every day without realizing it. Do you enjoy running, riding your bike and skipping? They are all good ways to keep fit.

Let's play leapfrog!

The more you use your body, the better it works.

Try some bending
and stretching
exercises.

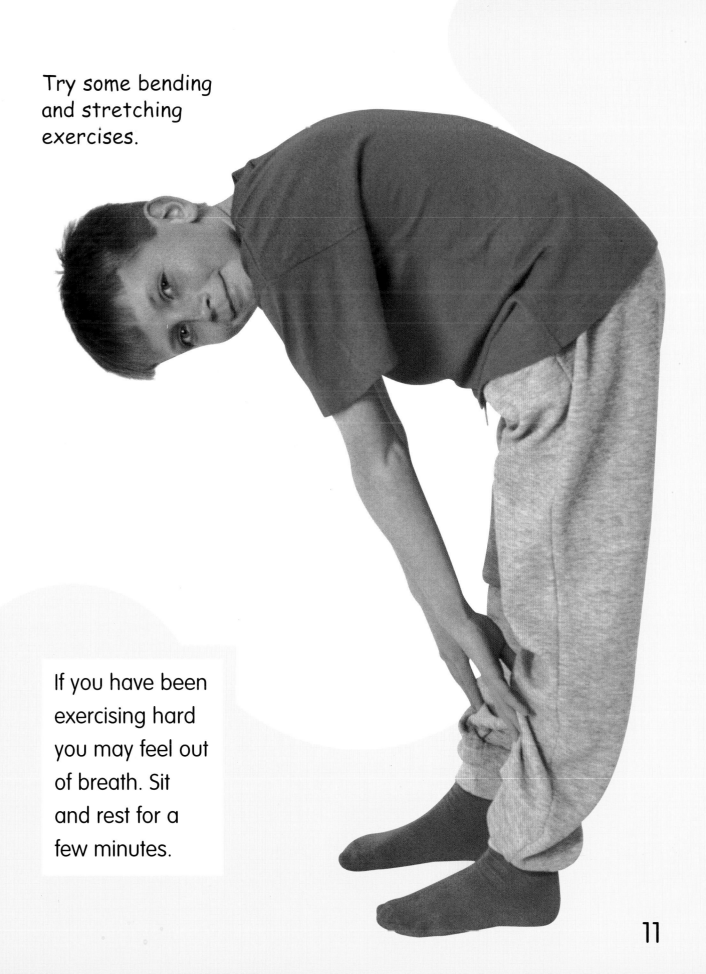

If you have been
exercising hard
you may feel out
of breath. Sit
and rest for a
few minutes.

Your skin

Your skin is very strong and hardwearing. It does an important job stopping harmful things, such as dirt and germs, getting inside your body.

pore   hair   skin surface

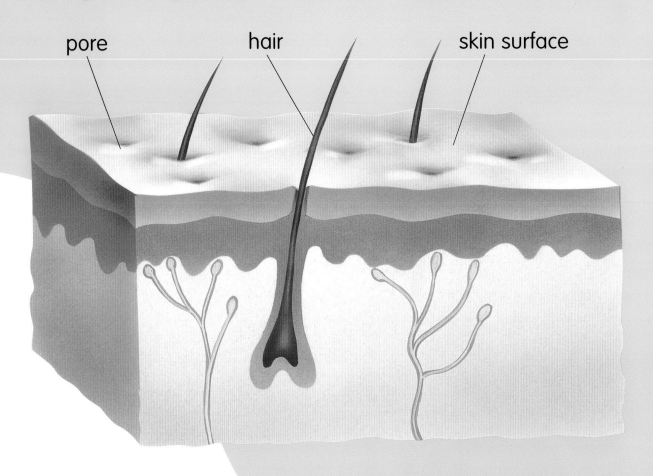

This is a drawing of your skin.

When you are cold, the hairs on your skin stand upright.

When you are
hot, sweat
comes out of
tiny holes in your
skin called pores.

Your skin is
soft, stretchy
and waterproof.

13

Keeping clean

Tiny things called germs are all around us. Most germs do not harm us, but some cause diseases. Washing with soap and water gets rid of dirt, germs and dead skin.

Always wash your hands when you have been to the toilet.

Germs are so tiny we cannot see them unless we look under a microscope.

If you do not wash, your skin will start to smell.

Your teeth

The teeth that begin to appear when you are about six years old will have to last you all your life, so look after them. Brush your teeth every day and try to visit the dentist every six months for a check-up.

Brush your teeth in the morning after breakfast and before you go to bed.

Too many sweets and
fizzy drinks can
cause tooth decay.

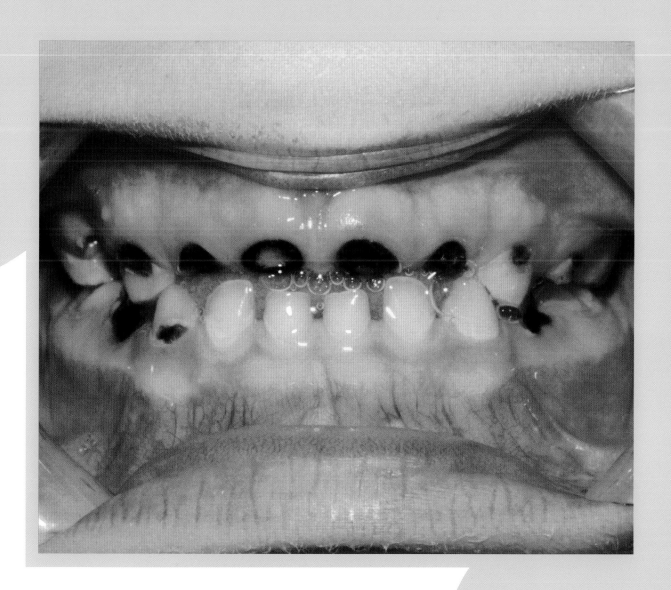

Crunchy vegetables like carrots
help to keep your teeth healthy.

Healthy hair

Hair needs to be washed every few days to keep it healthy. Washing your hair gets rid of dirt and dead skin cells and keeps it smelling clean and fresh.

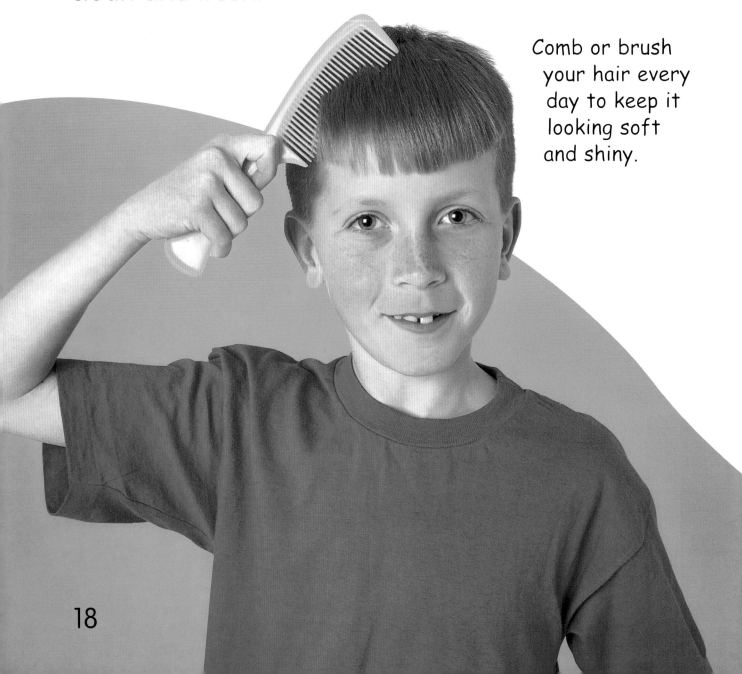

Comb or brush your hair every day to keep it looking soft and shiny.

Tiny insects called head lice can live in hair. This picture of a head louse is many times its real size!

If you have head lice, you will need to wash your hair with a special shampoo.

Falls and cuts

When you fall and hurt yourself, blood comes out of the wound. When the blood flow stops, the blood dries to form a scab. The scab stops germs getting into your body and making you ill.

A plaster will help keep out germs.

Clean the cut or graze
with water and dab on
antiseptic cream
or lotion.

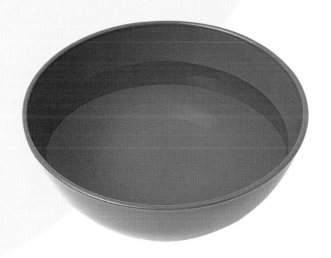

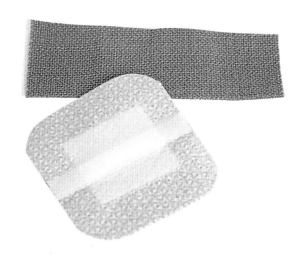

New skin grows
under the scab.
When the cut is
better the scab
will fall off.

Feeling ill

If germs get into your body they can make you feel ill. Germs that cause coughs and colds enter your body through your mouth and nose.

If you feel ill it is best to go to bed and keep warm.

If your illness doesn't go away, you may need to go and see the doctor.

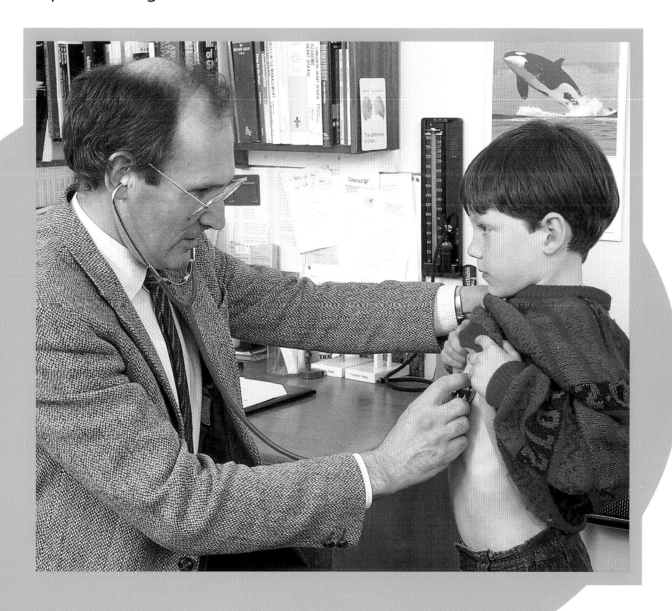

When you are ill, you feel tired. This is because your body is using its energy to fight off the germs.

Fighting diseases

Some diseases can be prevented by giving people injections or medicine to swallow. If you are ill you should stay at home so that you do not pass your illness on to other people.

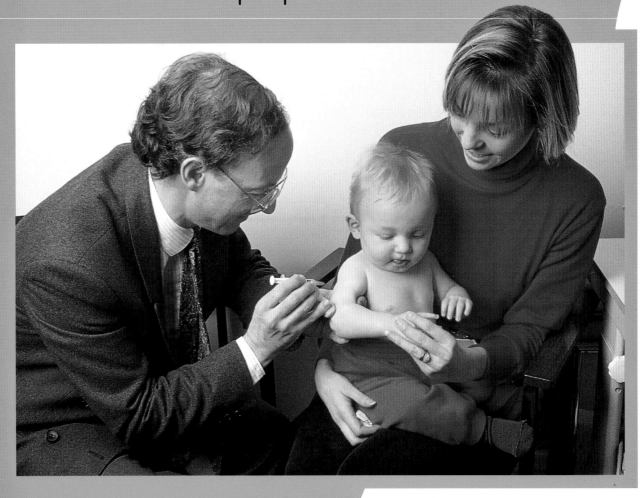

This baby is being given an injection.

Chickenpox is a disease that many people get when they are young.

When you sneeze, germs shoot into the air. Always sneeze into a handkerchief.

In the sun

It's great fun playing outdoors on a hot, sunny day, but too much sun can be bad for you. If you are sunburnt, your skin turns red and sore, and blisters may form.

Sitting in the shade helps to protect your skin.

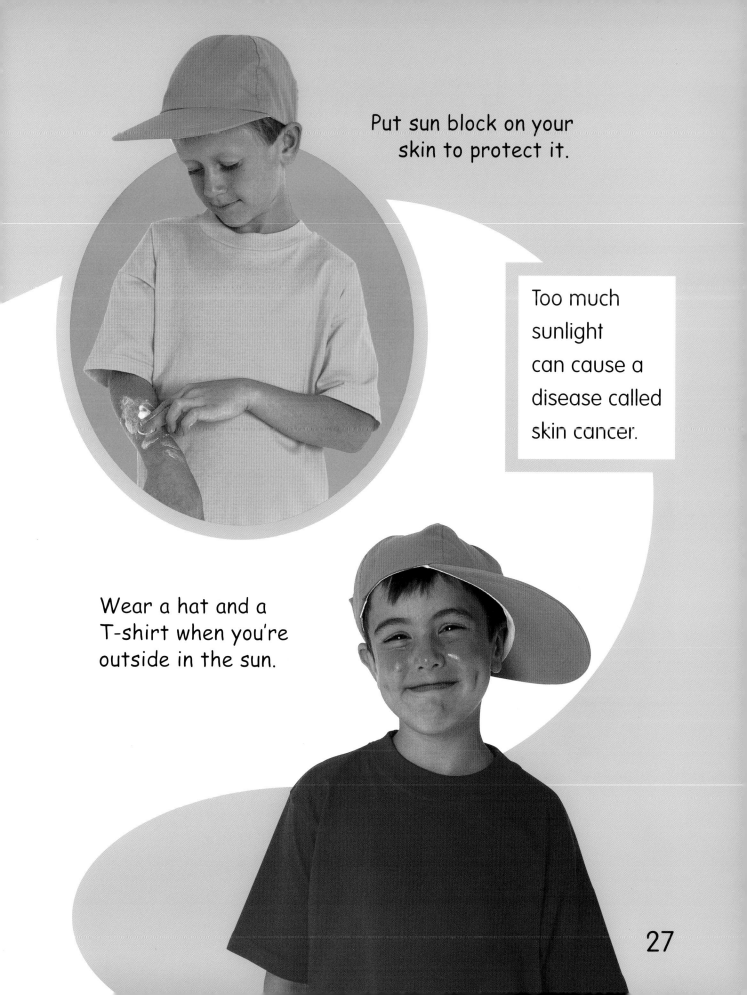

Put sun block on your skin to protect it.

Too much sunlight can cause a disease called skin cancer.

Wear a hat and a T-shirt when you're outside in the sun.

27

A clean home

Dusting, sweeping floors and vacuuming carpets gets rid of germs and helps to keep your home clean. Germs live in damp places, such as toilets and sinks, but they can be killed by special cleaners called disinfectants.

Keep the places where food is kept clean.

Washing clothes regularly keeps them fresh.

Always wash your hands before touching food.

Words to remember

antiseptic
A cream or liquid that kills germs.

blisters
Bubbles that form on burnt skin. Blisters can be very painful.

decay
To go bad or to rot.

disease
An illness. Chickenpox is a disease.

disinfectants
Special cleaners that can kill germs.

energy
The power you need to be able to work and play without feeling tired.

germs
Tiny things that are all around us. They can make you ill.

heart

The muscle inside your chest that pumps blood around your body.

injection

A way to protect people against diseases.

lungs

The two spongy areas in your chest that you use when breathing.

microscope

An instrument used by scientists to look at things that are very tiny.

muscles

Bundles of soft, stretchy fibres inside your body that make you move.

pores

Tiny holes in your skin.

sweat

Watery liquid that comes from your skin when you are very hot.

Index